Volume 6

BRITISH RAILWAYS IN COLOUR

Alan Earnshaw & Kevin Derrick

NORTH EASTERN
REGION

ARTHINGTON

Nostalgia Road Publications

The **British Railways In Colour** Series ™

is produced under licence by

Nostalgia Road Publications Ltd.

Unit 6, Chancel Place

Shap Road Industrial Estate, Kendal LA9 6NZ

Tel. 01539 738832 - Fax: 01539 730075

designed and published by
Trans-Pennine Publishing Ltd.
PO Box 10,
Appleby-in-Westmorland,
Cumbria, CA16 6FA
Tel. 017683 51053 Fax. 017683 53558
e-mail: admin@transpenninepublishing.co.uk

and printed by
Kent Valley Colour Printers Ltd.
Kendal, Cumbria
01539 741344

© Trans-Pennine Publishing Ltd. 2004
Photographs: As credited

Front Cover: The railways around Sunderland epitomise the very heart of the North Eastern Region, as exampled by Q6 0-8-0 63395, which is seen near Ryhope with a train of empty hoppers. *Strathwood Library Collection* (E371)

Rear Cover Top: This J72 0-6-0, 68723, displays the old North Eastern Railway livery as it brightens up Gateshead depot on a winter's day in 1962. *Strathwood Library Collection* (E346)

Rear Cover Bottom: At Ryhope Junction, a favourite spot for photographers, J27 65879 is seen in the midst of a forest of signals in 1967. *John Gleen* (E236)

Title Page: Seen scurrying through Arthington in July 1962, between Leeds and Harrogate, A4 4-6-2 60029 *Woodcock* leads the up Queen of Scots Pullman. This Pullman service via Harrogate was rostered for a Haymarket engine as far as Newcastle where a Neville Hill based A3 was the usual power on this leg in earlier years. We are 195 miles from Kings Cross at this point. *John Merritt* (E187)

This Page: Here we see a pair of Class J27 0-6-0s, 65892 and 65804, inside the grimy interior of the Sunderland (52G) roundhouse on 1st July 1967. *J. R. Beddows* (E301)

ALL RIGHTS RESERVED
No Part of this publication may be reproduced, stored in a retrieval system, or transmitted, in any form or by any means, electronic, mechanical, photocopying, recording or otherwise, without prior permission in writing from the publishers.
ISBN 1 903016 34 7
British Cataloguing in Publication Data
A catalogue record for this book is available from the British Library

WELCOME to the sixth volume of the **British Railways in Colour** series, which deals with the North Eastern Region. Although it was not created until 1956, it took over most of the railway territory that had been occupied by the pre-Grouped North Eastern Railway. It, like the North Eastern Region, had its headquarters in York, and once dominated the railway map of Northumberland, Durham, The North Riding of Yorkshire and a large part of the West Riding too. Between the Humber and the Tweed, it suffered very little in the way of incursion by 'foreign' railways, so (like the GWR) many of its practices, designs and activities continued unchanged through both the Grouping of 1923 and Nationalisation a quarter of a century later. Understandably, its autonomy was only to be expected, and it is only surprising that it took eight years to get it!

Above: *Although this picture at Newcastle Central dates from 1965, we find true echoes of the old North Eastern Railway with 68723. Rather than the drab BR un-lined black colour scheme, the J72 Class 0-6-0T has the pale green of the former North Eastern Railway and its crest in addition to the BR logo.*
Noel Marrison (E361)

The massive NER network had a mixture of both heavily industrialised areas and lightly populated countryside, and little changed in the mix after 1923. The addition of ex-Midland, LNWR, L&YR and GNR sheds brought about an eclectic mix of motive power when the new region was formed in 1956, but despite this NER-designed locomotives were in evidence down to the end of steam in 1967 as we will show in the pages that follow.

Above: The undoubted gem in the NER's crown was not the historic City of York, despite the fact that it had its imposing headquarters there, but the City of Newcastle-upon-Tyne. This was an industrial centre beyond compare, with coal mining, engineering, shipbuilding, maritime trade, steel and iron making and much more to provide traffic to the railways. Lines ran north, south, east and west, the latter going all the way through the Tyne Valley and over the Pennines to the City of Carlisle. Naturally, the station at the hub of this traffic, Newcastle Central, was very, very busy!

It is there that we see J72 Class 0-6-0T 68680, a long time Gateshead (52A) resident, on pilot duties in 1961. The J72s were eventually replaced with Class 03 or 04 0-6-0 diesel shunters which carried on this duty until the advent of the almost loco-less railway in the 1980s. The J72 design was built first by the NER in 1898 but later batches were added by both the LNER and BR up to 1951 and as such were unique in having a building span of 54 years. This particular example was scrapped at Darlington by May 1962. *John Gill* (E341)

Top Right: Along with York and Darlington stations, Newcastle Central was one of the three main hubs of the North Eastern Railway. Yet the location for the city's main station was one that would necessitate substantial civil engineering to reach, as it was located high above the River Tyne on its northern bank. Not one, but two major river crossings would eventually be built (High Level Bridge and the King Edward VII Bridge), and the station was built on a curve between these two. The complex junction point-work that resulted on what was a fairly cramped site became famous the world over. In 1961 we see A4 Glass 60014 *Silver Link* on the Elizabethan Express, with the castle in the background. The service will not stop at any one of Newcastle's 15 platforms, because when it was introduced in 1953 it became the world's longest daily non-stop (Edinburgh - London) run of 392.9 miles. *John Gill* (E325)

Bottom Right: Central Station was noted for its water columns to serve steam trains. These were located under the canopy extensions as can be seen here on 5th June 1965, as A3 Class 4-6-2, 60052 *Prince Palatine* is pictured taking on water. The engine carries a yellow cab-side warning stripe, which means it must not pass south of Crewe under the electric wires, but given that this engine is based at Edinburgh St. Margarets MPD (64A) only a special or rail tour would take it there! It should be remembered that Newcastle also had electric suburban train services as early as 1904. *Peter Coton* (E343)

Top Left: There was always a rich variety of motive power to be found in Newcastle, with most types being evident. The main exception was the BR standards, and the Britannia Pacifics were almost unheard of. The express passenger services were of course dominated by the big LNER Pacifics, with Gresley's smaller, mixed traffic V2 Class 2-6-2s undertaking a wide variety of duties. Here we see 60843 carefully setting back with a fitted van train at Newcastle Central in 1961. This is potentially a big problem at such a busy station, especially if something goes wrong on one of the many double slips. As can be seen above the locomotive, colour lights had already been introduced (at the end of the 1950s) in an attempt to simplify signal observance through the station. This picture, and others, was taken by a contributor who was stationed at one of the many RAF stations on the East Coast at this time. *John Gill* (E350)

Bottom Left: The non-stop workings through Newcastle were beautifully shown in the British Transport Film, *The Elizabethan* made in 1956. It made a star of 60017 *Silver Fox*, but here we see the train behind A4 4-6-2 60024 *Kingfisher*. This was one of the 23 (out of 34) locomotives in the class in British Railways days, that was fitted with a corridor tender, specially designed for these long runs. Note that *Kingfisher* has carried some extra embellishments since October 1954, with a decorative diamond shaped plaque depicting the bird from which the engine takes its name. *John Gill* (E357)

Above: A driver's eye view of the approach to a busy Newcastle Central Station on 2nd March, in the hard winter of 1963. Although the snows have gone, the steam and smoke from the double chimney of the A3 Pacific in the platform shows how cold the atmosphere is. One of the water columns mentioned earlier can be seen to the left, and it is unusually left extended out over the platform road - perhaps it is frozen in the adverse conditions?

With 15 platforms, serving a mixture of through, suburban, originating and terminating trains, Newcastle Central was a very busy location. Add to this the through coaches that had to be changed from one train to another, plus the parcels and mail vans that were handled, and you will appreciate why there was a need for a fleet of station pilots, like the J72s pictured earlier.
Strathwood Library Collection (E322)

Above: Colour photography in Northumberland is not at all common, especially on those rural lines away from the ECML. Wouldn't it be wonderful to find a collection of colour pictures on the line up to Alnwick, Wooler and Coldstream or the Amble branch? Even places like Bedlington, seen here on 21st June 1967, are relatively rare. Here we have a stranger to the NER, in the shape of one of the engines that came with the transfer of ex-LMS sheds in the West Riding in 1956. These Ivatt Moguls were introduced in 1947, with 43000 being the first of 162 power class 4 engines. It carried a double chimney when built, but later members of the class were built with a single chimney,

and the earlier ones were later re-built in that form. The North Eastern Region found its inherited 'flying pigs' to be very useful mixed traffic engines, but they used them extensively on coal trains. When others came available from the LMR, the NER were happy to offer them a home, this one migrated across the Pennines from Carlisle Kingmoor (12A) as late as December 1966. It was given a home at North Blyth (52F), where it stayed until the end of steam in the region on 1st September 1967. It then went to one of the smaller scrap metal contractors (Clayton & Davie at Dunston-on-Tyne), who set about scrapping her in November 1967. *John Gleen* (M462)

Above: Whilst the ex-LMS interlopers might have found gainful employment on the banks of the River Blyth, the traditional NER locomotive types were always ever present in what was a truly traditional North Eastern town. Although the port of Blyth dates from the 12th century, the modern town did not start to develop until the 18th century when a quay was erected for the shipment of coal. The port began to prosper after the Blyth Harbour & Dock Company was formed in 1853 and dredging allowed larger ships to enter the port and thus dramatically increase the amount of coal shipped out. By 1855, 250,000 tons of coal were being shipped and by 1900 this had increased to 3 million tons.

Blyth received its charter of 'Borough Status' in 1922 and by the 1950s the population had risen to 46,000. The 1950s saw a 'boom time' for coal-mining, shipbuilding and ship repair. Five coal mines were operating within a radius of two miles of the town centre, and a million tons of coal per year was being exported overseas from the port of Blyth, most of this coal being moved to the docks by rail. At this time 62% of the male workforce were employed in the mines while another 27% worked in the shipbuilding industry. Here K1 62024 is on the coaling stage ramp at North Blyth (52F) in July 1965, although by then it was officially a diesel shed. *Win Wall/Strathwood Library Collection* (E365)

Top Left: By 1961 Blyth was shipping more coal than any other port in Britain, and the link between the railways and the sea was more important than it had ever been. Indeed, few could tell that the prosperity it enjoyed would be completely decimated within two decades, as Britain completely turned its back on the traditional industries of coal, ship building and iron- and steel-making and the railways that served them. In happier days, a brace of Ivatt Moguls, 43008 and 43074, are found on the foreshore at North Blyth on 7th July 1967. Both are engaged on the light engine or brake van movements that were common in the coalfields. The benefits of the almost fully-enclosed cabs that were fitted to these tender engines is clearly to be appreciated, as Ivatt's design made tender-first running much easier. Whilst this may not have been a pre-requisite of the crew on a warm day in July, we can only imagine what it was like running tender-first with a J27 at such an exposed location in the middle of winter.
Dave Hill (M463)

Bottom Left: A pair of J27s, 65874 and 65819 are found in the straight shed at North Blyth in 1967. It seems that the main accessories for these engines was the shunter's pole on the front running plate. Obviously there was no need to return them to the stores each time, as was the case at some sheds. At some locations the crews would have to 'borrow' poles, lamps and oil cans from other engines so as to be ready for the road.
Noel Marrison (E355)

Top Right: As 1967 progressed, steam on the region went into decline, and North Blyth epitomises this melancholy era in a view taken there on 20th July 1967. As the day for their last trip to the scrapyard dawned, the lines of withdrawn engines grew and grew. Blyth was no different, and we see 65834, 65861, 43158, 43048, 62057, 43101 and 43012 bringing up the rear. We are grateful that the cameramen of the day took views such as these, for how many of us remember walking faithfully along the lines taking down the engines numbers for the last time.
John Gleen (E310)

Bottom Right: The disposal of the region's steam fleet saw the majority of engines being sold to local yards, where a voracious appetite for scrap saw the engines being cut up very quickly. One of these was the yard of Hughes Bolckow at Battleship Wharf, North Blyth, which was active between July 1964 and October 1967. In all 151 engines were dismantled, including A3 and A4 Pacifics before they went over to diesels and finally stopped railway work in 1968. Two of the common ex-NER victims were this J27, 65823 and its very rusty classmate seen at Thornaby (51L) on 29th January 1967. Interestingly 65823 contradicts the records as she looks to have already been out of traffic a while but was not withdrawn officially until March from Sunderland (52G) and then being stored at 52F North Blyth before the short shunt by diesel to Hughes Bolckow in the July.
J.R. Beddows (E315)

Above: South of the River Tyne, we find Gateshead (52A), one of the sheds that handed over a large number of its inhabitants to Hughes Bolckow. Included in the list were no less than four A1 Class 4-6-2s, these being 60116 *Hal o' The Wynd*, 60127 *Wilson Wordsell*, 60132 *Marmion* and 60142 *Edward Fletcher*. When they arrived at North Blyth they were in a dreadful state, but this is hardly surprising, as Gateshead had gained an unwanted reputation for the poor state its engines were turned out, even those on the named East Coast Main Line train workings. Yet this was not the case with all their engines.

Looking reasonably smart on 9th December 1962 this Gresley V3 2-6-2T, 67628, shows off her lined BR black livery and even the twin red boiler bands can be seen. These engines were then finding increasingly less work around Newcastle and were becoming confined to local newspaper and mail trains or empty carriage workings to and from Heaton. The arrival of diesel railcars did not put them straight into store as they had done with many other types, but nevertheless the V3s would not have much longer to keep going.
Noel Marrison (E329)

12

Top Right: Perhaps Gateshead's poor reputation was attributable to the fact that it was one of the sheds singled out for modernisation after the North Eastern Region was formed. During 1956 it started its slow transformation to a more modern shed as two of the former roundhouses were taken out of regular use. A more practical 70-foot turntable was installed and this allowed the Pacifics to come in from the cold at long last. Thereafter the cleaning of engines never seemed to be a high priority, yet as if to belie this fact, we have a remarkably clean Gresley A4 Pacific. Here 60009 *Union of South Africa* is on special duties and the 'new order' can be seen with Deltic D9001 *St. Paddy* lurking in the background. The depot was not officially closed to steam until the 30th March 1965, by which time its surviving Pacifics had been transferred to the Scottish Region.
Noel Marrison (E309)

Bottom Right: South of Gateshead and on the ECML mainline, we come to Low Fell as a V2 2-6-2 passes at great speed. Gresley designed this class for fast mixed traffic working and they performed this task admirably when properly maintained. Class member 60916 looks to be doing just that in the hands of a capable crew. There is a climb on the northbound lines at this point but most trains will have to slow for either the Newcastle stop or the host of junctions coming into view anyway. The run south had the benefit of the bank, but the slow climb back up to Chester-le-Street required a good run.
Noel Marrison (E348)

Top Left: Many photographers of the period were intent on recording what they could, but at the same time they were often hampered by a lack of personal transport. Accordingly, they made regular trips to their nearest possible vantage point and we therefore have many views of different engines at the same location; classic examples in our collection are places like Dore & Totley, Gamston Bank, Primrose Hill, Ryhope and here at Low Fell with 62041. *Noel Marrison* (E351)

Bottom Left: The assistance of the grade is seen again as a Q6 Class 0-8-0 63423 hustles past the same vantage point a few minutes later. For a power class 6 engine, the exhaust shows that very little steam is being consumed in keeping this short train on the move. Even though post-war housing in the Gateshead area increased considerably, Low Fell station was closed as early as 7th April 1952, nearby Bensham closed two years later and Lamesley had lost its passenger trains in 1945. Not far away a new marshalling yard (known as Tyne Yard) was being built at Lamesley. *Noel Marrison* (E345)

Right: When the BR Standard Class 9F 2-10-0s arrived on Tyneside to first supplement and then replace the O1s on the Consett trains, they quickly became popular with running crews and photographers alike. Their duties were not restricted to just the ore trains, but they could be found on many other workings too, such as the oil tank trains seen here at Low Fell in 1965. *Noel Marrison* (B281)

Above: For anyone visiting the town today, the role that Consett (or at least the Derwent Iron Works) played in the evolution of railway history would be hard to understand. Its passenger services on the Blackhill (Derwent Valley) line were withdrawn in April 1954, though the station remained notionally open until 23rd May 1955, when Consett's main station (on the 'deviation' line via Birtley and Leadgate) also lost its passenger trains. Even so, Consett was maintained as an 'un-staffed' halt for special passenger workings until 7th November 1960, and the remaining stub of the old Stanhope & Tyne Railroad stayed open to freight from the moorland terminus at Parkhead until April 1968.

Of course, the town will best be remembered for the steel works seen in the background of this picture, which developed from the old ironworks at Carr House. In turn they gave reason for the BR Standard 9F 2-10-0s that worked the iron-ore trains from Tyne Dock, and the coal trains that came up from the Durham coalfield; just look at all the empty mineral wagons to the top left of the picture. Still looking remarkably smart on 10th April 1965, Consett is pictured during the arrival of a special behind K1 Class 2-6-0 62027; we assume that the DMU on the adjacent platform was connected with the rail tour.

Strathwood Library Collection (E359)

Top Right: Consett will long be remembered by those who lived and worked there for the red haematite dust from the steel works that settled on the surrounding area. They will also long remember how Mrs. Margaret Thatcher set about a systematic demolition of Britain's steel industry and how it robbed the town of its principle employer. This saw the British Steel Plant being closed in 1980 and subsequently dismantled in what was (at the time) one of the largest demolition projects in Europe. Our view dates from a few years previously, when a Labour government was hastily dismantling the railway network, and removing steam from its lines. Here BR 9F 92064 shows off the two 10 inch Westinghouse air compressors that were fitted for working the dedicated wagons on the Tyne Dock - Consett ore trains. These were needed to maintain a pressure of 90psi during the loading procedures and for opening the wagon doors at Consett.
Brian Hopkinson (B282)

Bottom Right: Not too far to the east of Consett was the busy junction at Washington, which is pictured here on 4th May 1963 with a backdrop of miners' cottages. The ex-Ministry of Supply 8F, 90091, was used to working Welsh coal trains at Newport Ebbw Junction before being moved to Thornaby MPD (51L) on Teesside. Later she went to Goole (50D) to serve out her time on Yorkshire coal trains, before being sent for scrap to Drapers of Hull at the end of 1967.
Strathwood Library Collection (B289)

Top Left: Pelaw, east of Gateshead, was a name well known to travellers on the East Coast route, as it became part of the main line north of Washington in 1850. In so doing it superseded the old main line via Brockley Whinns, but its glory was short-lived, as in 1872 it too was replaced by a new line through the Team Valley. The first station closed in 1857 and the second one closed in November 1893 when a third station, Pelaw Junction, was built close to the site of the original station. From there three busy routes diverged, and to serve these lines BR installed a futuristic panel signal box along with the colour light signals. Here, K1 Class 62023 passes with yet another load of hoppers on 15th June 1967. By this date diesel classes 17, 24, 25, 27, 20, 37, 40, 46 and 47 could also be seen locally. If your interest strays to these you will be interested in our series on Heritage Traction covering *The Illustrated History of British Railways in Colour*.
Michael Beeton (E233)

Bottom Left: On the same day, Pelaw witnesses the passage of sister engine 62007 with a long rake of empty 21-ton coal hoppers on their way for another refill. Stop to wonder for a minute, just how many times one of these wagons would be used in its working life and how much coal it would have moved? Pelaw's station finally closed in 1979 following the opening of the Tyneside Metro, however things still looked promising when this picture was taken on 15th June 1967 even though steam in the region was fast coming to an end.
Michael Beeton (E238)

Above: The south bank of the Tyne to the east of Gateshead is clearly linked with the Newcastle & Darlington Junction Railway, The Stanhope & Tyne Railroad and the old colliery waggonways, but it is also closely associated with the co-operative movement. It was here that a vast group of factories were built between Shields Road and the railway by the Lancashire cooperative movement, as they endeavoured to spread the commercial principle of cooperative trading into the region at the turn of the century. In 1896 the Church Commissioners agreed to lease 3.75 acres of land between Heworth and Bill Quay to the Co-op for 999 years. This land lay conveniently between Shields Road and the North Eastern Railway, near Pelaw Junction.

The Co-operative Society, understandably, called its works by the name Pelaw, but before the factories were built, there was nothing between Heworth and Bill Quay except fields, the odd cottage, Catdean Burn, a few bridle paths and the Pelaw Main Waggonway. Within ten years a whole new community grew around the works, using the name Pelaw. By 15th June 1967 we can see the extent of urban growth as J27 65855 pauses for a signal. The crew are relaxed in the warm weather and the storm sheet is cast up onto the cab roof. Note the allotments that are to be seen in the background, which were then very popular and where potting sheds and greenhouses would spring up in some strange places.
Michael Beeton (E260)

Above: The exotic Stanhope & Tyne Railroad, which was promoted in 1831 and was bankrupt by the end of the decade had brave ideas of crossing the moors from Weardale to Derwentside, where it would carry limestone to the iron works at Carr House, and then take coal and pig iron to a new port on the Tyne. Indeed, by choosing not to follow the course of the old Derwent Valley waggonway, it was able to make for a new deep-water port nearer the mouth of the Tyne. The idea had instant appeal, as a new bridge that had just been built across the Tyne was already limiting the size of ships that could proceed beyond Gateshead. The problems with construction costs and the difficulties of operating a railway with numerous rope-worked inclines (all of which had differing capacities) proved to be its downfall. Of course, in the longer term, the railways proved to be very resilient, and in the years that followed the S&T formed the basis of a busy route from North West Durham to Tyne Dock. Yet busy locations like Tyne Dock and Tyne Yard are locations where it seems hard to find colour photographs of steam locomotives. Therefore, this 1965 shot of stovepipe chimney V2 Class 60813 at Tyne Yard is all the more appreciated for the rarity of the location. An experiment from a time when steam was still considered to have a future, it was just one of the many variations that existed within the class of 184 V2 engines.
Noel Marrison (E362)

Below: Interestingly, the S&T had built its line by 'way-leaves' and agreed private rental agreements with the landowners, rather than obtain an Act of Parliament, which would have revealed its true (and extremely exorbitant) construction costs. The 'way-leaves' were inexpensive across the moors, but the Church Commissioners owned a massive 'ransom strip' as the line neared the coast, and they saw the opportunity to milk the situation for what it was worth. A revitalised S&T was formed in the shape of the Pontop & South Shields Railway in 1842, but it only took on the railway from Carr House down to Tyne Dock, and it was left to the Derwent Iron Company to re-open the moorland section over to Stanhope.

The P&SSR later became part of the NER and its difficult inclines were deviated, a new $6^1/2$-mile route was opened in 1896 between the S&T at Consett and the ECML north of Chester-le-Street. Tyne Dock MPD grew in importance as a result. We see it here in 1965 as a pair of the two-cylinder Q6s (63344 and 63387) pose out of service by the engine lifting apparatus. This piece of equipment pre-dated the hydraulic units (that dropped wheels into a service pit below the engine) and involved lifting the entire engine so that the wheels could be dropped from the lifted frames. It was all very basic and dated from the 1870s, having been supplied by Cowans Sheldon of Carlisle.
Win Wall, Strathwood Library Collection (E349)

Above: In addition to the two-cylinder Q6 0-8-0s at Tyne Dock, there was an allocation of three-cylinder Q7 0-8-0s that were used to bank the heavy ore trains on the stiff grades up to Consett. They were in constant use during World War II, but after nationalisation engines such as 63468 were booked to carry out around three banking duties per shift. The timings on the Consett route from Tyne Dock allowed just under two hours for the steeply graded route. These were powerful locomotives with an 8F power classification that were therefore used to the full capacity on most of their duties. The work of bankers was later shared by ex-WD 8Fs and (as seen here) by BR Standard 9Fs
John Gill (E222)

Right: The arrival of the 9Fs at Tyne Dock (originally coded 54B but changed to 52H before closure) was at first intended to supplement the older LNER engines, but they very soon came to replace them. They were soon mastered by local crews, and they could have been kept working long after the date of their withdrawal on 1st September 1967. A Sunday visit to the shed four years earlier would perhaps find four 9Fs such as 92065 and 92066 (with 92097 and 92064 out of camera) as they waited for another ship of Scandinavian iron ore to be unloaded so that they could shift it from the port up the stiff climb that led to the moorland town of Consett.
Strathwood Library Collection (B207)

Top Left: Thus far we have mostly mentioned the River Tyne and the relationship between the region's railways and the trans-shipment of coal on to maritime vessels. Yet, from 1693 onwards a series of waggonways began linking coal mines to the River Wear. Improvements with steam engines and iron rails came as early as 1822 with George Stephenson's Hetton Colliery Railway, as the Wear came to be part of the cradle of the railways. As Sunderland's rail network grew, it assumed a massive socio-economic role in the development of heavy industry (including shipbuilding) on Wearside. Here we see a local stalwart, a J27 Class 0-6-0, 65894.
Strathwood Library Collection (E200)

Bottom Left: The skyline of Sunderland in the distance with another J27 from Percy Main shed (52E) this time engaged in shunting the yard. Much of Sunderland has been swept aside as industry is, according to the buzz-words of the day, modernised, downsized, economised or just plain shut down.
Len Smith (E302)

Right: Here a pair of J27's are found, 65833 and an anonymous class member that has lost its smokebox door plate, in Sunderland's roundhouse. Also lurking inside the unglamorous shed on that sunny day in 1965 was 65892. All three engines showed the heavy burning that was a common sight on engines working in the Durham coalfields at that time.
Win Wall,
Strathwood Library Collection (E240)

Top Left: Typical of those railways that originated coal destined for Sunderland was the Silksworth branch, and in later years it became a favourite location for many enthusiasts to watch trains from the vantage of a hilltop or spoil heap. One such example is well into the climb on that line's distinctive embankment in 1966. If the gradient had faced the other way, loaded trains on this line would most likely have been one of the many (and sadly missed) rope-worked inclines. All of these colliery branches had a real character about them and many enthusiasts will fondly recall visiting them, as they were so full of interest. The trackwork was often very basic and this was compounded by little or no maintenance and regular subsidence. Derailments were frequent as a result, but they were often quickly fixed by experienced crews who knew how to drag wagons over chocks to get things going again.
Dave Hill (E283)

Bottom Left: Our attention now turns south of Sunderland to Ryhope Grange, which was one of those locations that was well photographed in the last years of steam. Here the fireman of J27 65882 gets out to inspect the outbreak of a potential lineside fire, as we can see from the smoking embankment to the far left of the picture. Although, for someone who spends his working day stoking fires, quite how good his efforts will actually be at putting them out is not clear. Still it is a nice day and who knows they may have sent up a few cinders of their own earlier.
Michael Beeton (E288)

Top Right: The same lineside fire at Ryhope Grange is apparently being ignored by the crew of J27 65892, which is seen running tender-first with a train of loaded hopper wagons. During the hot summer of 1967, fires such as this were very common, especially in the bramble bushes to be found on most linesides. Most permanent way men saw these fires as a good way of keeping down the undergrowth, but after that summer lineside fires would become a very rare thing after steam was withdrawn from the region. This engine was to go out of traffic six weeks later anyway, and closure notices for the steam sheds had already been posted.
Michael Beeton (E327)

Bottom Right: Some of the drivers had begun learning the ways of the English Electric (Class 37) diesels, but many more would be forced to retire to their allotments or tend their pigeons or grow specimen vegetables. That last summer is full of mixed emotions for those that experienced the lineside, for here the workaday steam engine was coming to its end; it died as it had been born, moving coal from colliery to coast. Those enthusiasts who were pre-occupied with chasing the last runs of Bullieds and Standards on the Southern in the summer of 1967 certainly missed something in the North Eastern Region. As 65804 runs on to the Ryhope embankment on 14th June 1967, it is worth reflecting that, by this stage the J27 Class were the oldest working locomotives on British Railways. *Michael Beeton* (E358)

Top Left: The early lines in Wearside all ran west - east, taking coal from the pits to the ports, and a north - south coastal railway did not develop for many years. Even the Durham & Sunderland Rly, opened in 1836, did not buck the general trend. A north-south 'coastal' line was finally achieved by an amalgam of various railways culminating with the Londonderry Railway from Seaham to Ryhope Grange Junction, and a new NER line from Ryhope Grange into Sunderland. Stopped on the bank at Ryhope Grange, is K1 Class 2-6-0 62060 which has been running tender-first. It has a loaded train made up of mixed 16- and 21-ton wagons with one of the once common 21-ton brake vans. A carefree fireman has not put down the water filler cover on the tender.
Michael Beeton (E316)

Bottom Left: The importance of the railway south of Ryhope Grange Junction cannot be underestimated, and its role in the history of coal movement is therefore highly significant. On 14th June 1967 we see one such movement behind Riddles 2-8-0 90348, which is still very much earning her keep with a train of empty 21-ton hoppers. These wagons were introduced by the LNER long before the war, as a way of increasing train loadings without the deadweight of extra wagons. Yet, in their design, these hoppers (mostly built at Shildon) still owed much to the original wooden chaldron waggons that were long used in the Durham coalfield, as they operated by the principle of top loading and gravity-assisted bottom discharge.
Michael Beeton (B219)

Above: Another view of the same 8F Riddles WD/MoS designed locomotive 90348 as it makes its way along the coast near Ryhope in July 1967. This was one of many similar locomotives that were transferred up to the North East in order to get a final year or so out of them. Their duties would almost exclusively be on coal trains around Hartlepool and Sunderland. This particular example had found its way to Sunderland (52G) after the end of steam at Wakefield (56A) and the opening of a new diesel depot at Healey Mills. For most of their BR lives engines such as this would be seen at the head of coal trains, but here we capture it with an unfitted LMS brake van in tow, possibly en-route to collect a train.

It was 'light' movements such as this that Beeching wanted to eliminate from the railways, and ultimately the Merry-Go-Round principle of operation would be developed. But back in the 1960s there were limits on what could be safely taken up and down those rickety colliery branches without the costly upgrading of track. These problems were not solved with dieselisation, but today's modern high capacity coal wagons, run on far superior permanent way, although to fewer destinations as the coal industry itself has been virtually decimated. Sadly, 90348 has only another couple of months to work, and then a fast sale to Hughes Bolckow at North Blyth would see her reduced to a pile of scrap and written off as an asset. *Dave Hill* (B237)

Above: As mentioned earlier, the Hetton area provided some of the region's most significant early steam railways, and the five Stephenson locomotives supplied for the Hetton to Sunderland Railway have a special place in railway history. The line from South Hetton to Seaham Harbour also continued the west-east trend of colliery lines in the area. By the 1870s, the NER needed to fill in the gaps between the Wear and the Tees, and in 1872 a new line was authorised between Stockton (Bowesfield Junction) and the line that ran from West Hartlepool to Sunderland at Wellfield. It was opened in two sections, Bowesfield to the Clarence Railway at Carlton West in May 1877, and from Carlton to Wellfield in March 1880.

It is at Wellfield that we see a Railway Correspondance & Travel Society railtour in 1963, behind one of the powerful three-cylinder Raven Q7 Class 0-8-0s. As these were then disappearing fast, the survivors, such as 63460 were frequently rostered for special excursions to lines that had long since lost regular stopping passenger trains. This one heads what is believed to be the last passenger train to call at Wellfield, which had already closed back on 9th June 1952 along with Thornley, Shotton Bridge, Haswell and South Hetton; however, these stations lasted longer than their counterparts south of Wellfield (Hurworth Burn and Wynyard), which lost their passenger trains in the Depression of 1931. *Noel Marrison* (E347)

Above: Not far to the east of Wellfield, the Castle Eden line was another of those west-east railways. This started life as a mineral branch of the Hartlepool Dock & Railway to Wingate, where it was later joined in an end-on junction by an $8^{1}/_{2}$ mile line from Ferryhill. Rejoicing in the grand title of The Great North of England, Clarence & Hartlepool Junction Railway, it opened between Wingate and Kelloe Bank in March 1839, but it was not until 1846 that passenger trains were working between Ferryhill and Hartlepool. Although the line was leased by George Hudson in 1848, the Great North of England, Clarence & Hartlepool Junction remained a nominally independent railway until the Grouping in 1923.

The line lost its passenger trains in 1952, but the collieries kept on providing the traffic. Very few of the coal mines had any method of turning an engine, although some did have triangular junctions nearby. In the absence of turning facilities, tender-first workings were common, and this tempted many photographers to capture the scene during the 1960s. Fortunately they can share it with us many years later, and a classic example, WD 2-8-0 90014, is captured at work on 27th June 1966. It has just left the junction at Hart and attacks the 1 in 70 grade as it heads inland with empty mineral 16-ton wagons destined for one of the collieries on the Castle Eden branch.

John Newman (E307)

Above: Hartlepool and West Hartlepool were once separate boroughs, and the two did not come together until 1967, the year in which steam ended in the region. The first line to reach the area was another of those west - east lines, the Clarence Railway, which was designed to challenge the Stockton & Darlington by opening a post nearer to the estuary of the River Tees. The Clarence worked very closely with the Stockton & Hartlepool Railway and was later absorbed by them .

The development of the small fishing port of Hartlepool and its associated railway network is a long story, but it is worth recalling that there was no direct link between Hartlepool and Sunderland until 1905, when a new line was opened from Hart to Seaham, taking over the Londonderry Railway in the process. On 16th June 1967 we find ourselves in the town's main station as WD 2-8-0 90698 psses through on the sharp curve.

Michael Beeton (B231)

Below: Hartlepool MPD (51C) was one of those sheds that only knew hard work, and it had few glamorous turns as it served the heavy coal mining and maritime industries that prevailed locally. Its allocation of engines reflected this, and any visit was sure to be rewarded by the sight of engines that had paint blistered away from their smokeboxes in mute testimony of their arduous lives. Towards its end it was an easy shed to gain access to, and as its entrance was just a short walk from the station it became very popular with visitors.

A little variety is supplied in this 1965 view by the Peppercorn-designed K1 Class 2-6-0, 62045 from Darlington (51A). These popular Moguls were a common sight on the railways of Durham and several of them managed to hang on to the end, of these 62005 became a rail tour favourite (as we will later see in this book) and it thankfully went into preservation. One of the ever-present WD 2-8-0s stands in the background, but the shed housing it will close to steam on 1st September 1967.

Len Smith (E253)

Top Left: There was some intensive working of the two lines between Sunderland and Hartlepool, with the original inland line via Murton, Haswell and Wellfield and the coastal line of 1905 both being in constant use. As mentioned, tender-first running was really quite commonplace as we see on 13th June 1967, when we view 90135 from Sunderland (52G) rounding the many curves around Hartlepool. This shot well illustrates the benefit given to the footplate crew by the design of the cut back bunker on Riddle's tender. They were designed like this to assist in their service in Europe at the end of World War II, as it was conceived that all the turntables could have been destroyed by the retreating German occupation forces.
Michael Beeton (B227)

Bottom Left: When the 'new line' opened between Seaham and Hart in 1905, fast trains could finally avoid the climb up Hesleden Bank in one direction and Seaton Bank in the other. Even so at least one LNWR/NER Liverpool-Newcastle express continued to use the old route for a number of years. The route north from Wellfield was the preserve of freight traffic after passenger trains were withdrawn in the early 1950s, but this remained an attractive run through some pretty countryside. With its brakes pinned down hard this J27 will be doing its best with only the engine brake and brake van to hold back the rake of hopper wagons behind it creeping slowly down Seaton Bank in 1966.
Dave Hill (E305)

Above: We have already briefly mentioned, that the railway to Port Clarence was intended to compete with the Stockton & Darlington. Yet, at the same time the Clarence was hamstrung by the fact that it had to send its traffic along a good part of the S&D, as it was not allowed to develope a truly independent and competing line. The Clarence also had its sights set on serving the coal mining district around Crook in South West Durham, as well as the lead-mining and limestone producing valley of Weardale beyond. Once the Clarence had become part of the Stockton & Hartlepool, it became something of a backwater, although part of it did become a section of the NER's electrified route from Shildon to Newport-on-Tees.

Passenger services on the stub from Billingham to Port Clarence were handed over to a pair of NER petrol-electric railcars in December 1904, and the experiment was such that steam railcar operation was commenced the following year and remained active until the 1920s. After the Grouping locomotive-hauled stock was used, but the passenger service was withdrawn as a wartime economy measure on 11th September 1939. Twenty-three years later, on 13th October 1962, B16/3 Class 4-6-0 61418 has ventured down the branch with an enthusiasts' special. The engine also had very little time left in service, as it was withdrawn in June 1964 and scrapped at Drapers four months later. *Strathwood Library Collection* (E360)

Top Left: Teesside, with its mass of lines on either bank of the river was, of course, the objective of the Stockton & Darlington Railway that opened in 1825. As the world's first public railway it was not slow to capitalise on its success, and as the town of Stockton found its shipping facilities increasingly inadequate, the railway was promoted over the river in 1830. A new town emerged on the mud flats of the south bank, and Middlesbrough was born. Across the river from the original S&DR terminus was the township of Thornaby, and it gave its name to the station known as South Stockton prior to 1893. A major railway centre evolved here, and it is at Thornaby MPD (51L) we now see A8 Class 69860, designed as a 4-4-4T for the NER by Sir Vincent Raven in 1913 and modified to a 4-6-2T by Gresley in 1931. On 6th September 1959 it faces an uncertain future, and along with a J72 and another A8 it has been stored at Thornaby shed having been displaced by the arrival of Metropolitan Cammell railcars a few months earlier. *Strathwood Library Collection* (E323)

Bottom Left: Freight of course was always Teesside's reason for being and we now visit Thornaby Station on 11th April 1959. There we see 90373, which is just one of many hundreds of these hard working Ministry of Supply or War Department locomotives that spent the bulk of their post-war lives both working in the region and becoming synonymous with it. We would be very interested to hear from readers who photographed this area in colour. *Strathwood Library Collection* (B207)

Above: A much more glamorous locomotive A4 Pacific 60004 *William Whitelaw* has stopped for a photo opportunity during a rail tour at Eaglescliffe in July 1963. Sadly the view is somewhat marred by the fact that the access flaps in the streamlined casing have been left unsecured. This was quite typical of the practice on Gresley 'Streaks' at that time, and not only did they rattle quite conspicuously when travelling at speed, they also spoilt photographs when they were stopped. The pronounced pimple effect at the top of the casing is also noticeable in this view, as is the double blast pipe chimney that was fitted to this class in the late 1950s. Sadly one of the region's main sheds at that time, Gateshead (52A) did nothing to help their appearance and it had an appalling reputation for the cleanliness of its roster of A4 Pacifics.

Eaglescliffe was fortunate to be served by two railways, one of which was the Stockton & Darlington and the other being the Leeds Northern. When it opened in 1852 much of the old S&DR route between Eaglesfield and Stockton was abandoned and the track re-aligned to run parallel to the Leeds Northern. It was also near Eaglesfield, on the section of track from Oak Tree Junction, that the famous Stockton & Darlington Centenary Procession was held in 1925. Fittingly the last exhibit in the procession of 53 engines and trains was the line's first locomotive, *Locomotion No.1*, which appeared to be running under its own steam. However, the LNER had cunningly disguised a petrol engine inside the tender and the smoke that belched from the chimney was just from oily rags that were being burnt within. *Trans Pennine Archive* (E303)

Above: Whereas Eaglescliffe was a meeting point between the Stockton & Darlington Railway and a main line from the south, Darlington was where two lines crossed at right angles. In a future volume in this series we intend to look at the East Coast Main Line in detail between York and Darlington, so our consideration of these two important railway centres in this book is somewhat limited. Even so, this was the very birthplace of the world's public railways, and Darlington is unique. Today an excellent museum is found in North Road Railway Station on the old S&DR, but it is on the other route, the line from York to Newcastle that the town's main railway station developed at Bank Top.

Bank Top was of course synonymous with the Gresley A4 Pacifics, and perhaps the most famous of them all 60022 *Mallard* is found at Darlington. The scene is set in the days before green 'wellies' and Barbour jackets became the vogue, and in the snows of January 1963 good old-fashioned black Wellington boots and a duffle coat were considered ideal garb for train spotting. Although *Mallard* would ultimately be preserved, by the time this picture was taken the first five A4s had been withdrawn from King's Cross a couple of weeks earlier. By the end of the year just 19 A4s would be left, and the survivors would be sent to Scotland. *Strathwood Library Collection* (E264)

Top Right: Steam still had some time to live at Darlington however, and we find an ex-works Stanier 8F fresh off North Road Works hiding inside Darlington shed. Outside, enjoying the summer weather is a reasonably clean A1 Class Pacific, 60145 *St. Mungo*, without a yellow stripe down the cab side. Yet the early 1960s were also a time of change as the railway workshops were mainly concentrating on building new diesel locomotives and scrapping redundant steam engines. Darlington disposed of hundreds of engines, but when this picture was taken on 4th June 1965, such work had ceased at Darlington 15 months earlier. The maintenance on steam engines was still being continued, but sadly the days of the works were numbered and it would close in April 1966.
Peter Coton (E308)

Bottom Right: After the war, the cash-strapped LNER picked up no less than 75 0-6-0STs to a design introduced by R.A. Riddles for the Ministry of Supply in 1943. With cessation of hostilities the LNER acquired them in 1946 and they entered service as the J94 Class. One of these, 68043, is seen here with the cooling towers of Darlington Power Station as its background. These 0-6-0STs were built by a number of different manufacturers, including several in the North East that normally specialised in building industrial types. As a result there could be significant differences between the various members of the J94 Class and the most noticeable was the hopper bunker carried by several of them. *Peter Coton* (E321)

Above: The original terminus of the Stockton & Darlington Railway was at Witton Park at the bottom of Weardale, but the secondary goal of the scheme was the mineral-rich dale itself. Local deposits of iron, lead and above all limestone were in high demand to feed the burgeoning industry of Teesside. A series of extensions took the railway up to Wearhead in 1895, but the principle town in Weardale, Stanhope, was reached in 1862. When the line to Wearhead opened a new station was built at Stanhope, but passenger services only lasted up to 29th June 1953. Ten years later, on 28th September 1963, a railtour arrived at the town behind named B1 61037 *Jairou*.
Strathwood Library Collection (E84)

Right: Due to a high ridge of Magnesian Limestone between Shildon and South Church, Bishop Auckland did not get its railway until 1842/3, but the town's station grew to become an important junction. On 25th September 1963 it was to host a rail tour behind Q7 Class 63460, seen running round her train. These tours always had plenty such stops for the travellers to get out and explore (some times for the first and last time) the rather remote spots being visited. The crew and inspector saw to the formalities of the engine's needs, and as the guard looked after the train as the passengers explored. However, shots such as this one without any human intrusion are rare.
Strathwood Library Collection (E311)

Above: Another rail tour arrives at a line that has clear associations with George Stephenson and the early days of railways. The Whitby & Pickering scheme opened fully as a west-east route in 1836. Stephenson had become involved in the choice of route in 1832 and he had advocated the benefits of the traffic links that would come from a railway serving the busy port of Whitby. It opened to Grosmont in June 1835, as the line climbed steadily from the coast, following first one bank of the River Esk and then the other. Beyond Grosmont a ridge provided a major obstacle, and a short tunnel took it out of the Esk Valley. To enable it to reach the plateau at Goathland the next section of track included a rope-worked 1:15 incline almost a mile long.

Today the area around Grosmont and Goathland is famous as the setting for the TV series Heartbeat and also for the wonderful North Yorkshire Moors Railway. However, back on 1st October 1963 there were few thoughts of preservation. Our picture does however, show enthusiasts at Grosmont, where another special has arrived with two B1 4-6-0s in charge; these were both named engines, 61018 *Gnu* and 61031 *Reedbuck*. Camping coaches can be seen to the right on the Egton curve, whilst the classic hipped North Eastern Railway signal box is in a good position to see all that it controls. Many details are to be seen by the careful observer or modeller.

Strathwood Library Collection (E83)

Below: Whitby was the ultimate goal of no less than lines from four directions. In addition to the lines from Pickering and Middlesbrough, which terminated along the side of the River Esk, the coastal line from Scarborough to Teesside called at a station located on the West Cliff. That line had a spur down to the low level route along the Esk, but despite being one of the most scenically attractive coastal railways in Britain, Whitby West Cliff lost its passenger services in 1961. Sadly the tourism appeal of the Yorkshire Coast was waning as foreign holidays came into vogue during the 1960s, and those who did come to explore Captain Cook's home port and the 'birthplace of 'Dracula' increasingly arrived not by railway, but motor coach or car. Even the move to DMU services did not stem the flow and Beeching proposed the closure of all lines to Whitby, however the Middlesbrough line was reprieved on the grounds of social necessity. Whitby was nevertheless a popular destination, and here it is being visited by one of the great pioneers of the early preservation scene, the late Lord Garnock's K4 Class 2-6-0, *The Great Marquess*, which is seen here carrying its former LNER green livery and the number 3442.
Trans Pennine Archive (E356)

Left: A popular holiday venue further down the East Coast, which promised fun and laughter whatever the weather, was Billy Butlin's holiday camp at Filey. It was even provided with its own station, which is where we see our old friend K1 62005 working with 3442 on a rail tour. The branch finally gave up at the end of the 1977 holiday season, unable to compete against the onslaught of cars and foreign air travel then becoming more easily affordable.
Trans Pennine Archive (E304)

Above: On the same tour, but further south at Bridlington, we see the pair (62005 and 3442) drawing a crowd as they take on water from a truly classic and elegant water column. From this view it is obvious that back in the 1960s young lads still wore short trousers and long socks even on cold days, which is a far cry from the trainers and baseball caps of today. Camera cases were in brown leather and fur coats were a desirable fashion statement for the ladies.
Trans Pennine Archive (E313)

Above: Perhaps the greatest of the East Coast ports were those situated on the River Humber, with Hull being the primary one. Fishing, general cargo and even North Sea ferries were the staple trade of the port, whilst Grimsby across the river became legendary for its fishing fleet. In the 1960s the Port of Hull was a very important part of Britain's economy, and we are keen to hear from photographers that took colour pictures there. The story of railways around the Humber deserves to be more fully told in a separate volume, so for the moment we are offering a taster of what life was like there back in the days of steam. To do so, we present a series of images taken in the cavernous interior of Hull Dairycoates MPD (53A later 50B).

Underlining the previously stated proliferation of the Riddles 8F locomotives in the North East, we see 90378 and 90695 beside the now preserved B1 61306, as they rest in the roundhouse at Dairycoates. Many of these WD/MoS engines met their end in Hull, and the yard at Dairycoates was eventually to become a holding ground for many of these 2-8-0s; indeed over two hundred went for scrap locally. Imagine, had Drapers of Hull become a safe haven like Woodhams yard in Barry, we would have 2-8-0s on every preserved line today! Ironically the pair seen here both went, not to Drapers but to the Hughes Bolckow's yard at North Blyth two years later in 1967.
Win Wall/Strathwood Library Collection (B220)

Top Right: Here 61306 is seen on the same visit to Dairycoates by our photographer in 1967. This is not long after the arrival of the D95xx 0-6-0 diesels built at Swindon a couple of years earlier, but by then unwanted by the Western Region. They would find sanctuary by ousting many of the National Coal Board's steam fleet at locations such as Philadelphia and Ashington on the North Eastern Region. Whilst the Thompson B1, a native of the North East, would initially find a place in that haven for Stanier's 4-6-0s on the London Midland at Carnforth. Before preservation 61306 would end a long spell as a Hull regular with a four-month stint at Low Moor (56F) until October 1967, the last two months stored there after the shed's closure.
Win Wall,
Strathwood Library Collection

Bottom Right: The awakening of an alternative kind of photography and with the classic work of Colin Gifford that appeared in many publications of the day, several photographers were led to experiment in capturing scenes that were different from the traditional three-quarter portrait. The sheds and roundhouses of the North East were to tempt many to persevere with views of sunlight and dancing patterns across engines that would otherwise be impossible to capture in a traditional view. In this style Dairycoates shed holds a pair of Austerities in 1965, with 90009 being prominent.
Win Wall,
Strathwood Library Collection (B180)

Above: There can be no doubt that York has always been a prominent staging point on the main transport routes passing east to west and north to south through Yorkshire. The Romans and the Vikings both had large settlements there, making much use of the navigable River Ouse passing through the city centre. In later years, a regular stagecoach and waggon service plied between York and London, but a railway was not to come in the first tranche of building. Indeed, it was the formation of the North Midland scheme from Derby to Leeds that ultimately led to creation of the York & North Midland Railway in October 1835, and its proposals to build a line from the city to join the NMR at Normanton.

The first section opened to Milford in May 1839, where a connection was made with the Leeds & Selby Rly., whilst the rest of the route opened in 1840. York's prosperity as a rail centre was then assured. Lines radiated in all directions, but it was of course the development of the East Coast Main Line between Edinburgh and London that ensured the success. One hundred and twenty four years later, in 1963, the massive station complex that developed is seen as Thompson A1 Class Pacific, 60124 *Kenilworth*, drifts back light engine. The need for express oil lamps on top of the electric lights fitted to this locomotive is an untidy necessity for the benefit of signalmen in daylight.
Trans-Pennine Archive (E199)

Below: The growth of York, the North Midland Railway and in turn, the North Eastern Railway, was primarily due to one man. George Hudson is one of the undisputed characters of the railway age, and his flair for overcoming or manipulating his competitors was seen with the Leeds & Selby, which he acquired in November 1840 and thereafter managed to dictate just which routes passenger and goods trains would take. A line to Scarborough, first proposed as early as 1833, was authorised by Parliament on 4th July 1844 and opened just 368 days later. The following year, 1845, saw a line promoted east from Church Fenton to Harrogate, but the most important link was the Great North Of England Railway that opened a route through the Vale of York to Darlington in 1841.

The railway that developed in York built not only a magnificent station, but also a grand hotel and some wonderful offices. The main one of these, Hudson House, still bears the name of the man who became better known as the 'Railway King'. What a pity the name was not bestowed on one of Gresley's A4 Pacifics, as these enjoyed names associated with lesser known railway servants, such as Walter K. Whigham. It was he who gave his name to the LNER 4487 *Sea Eagle* in October 1947. With its BR number of 60028 it is seen on York MPD (50A) in 1961. It was one of the many A4s withdrawn in January 1963, and prompted many enthusiasts to capture their last days in colour, even so 60001 *Sir Ronald Matthews* is particularly rare; unless you know better? *John Gill* (E254)

Top Left: In March 1942, during World War II, the Luftwaffe were ordered to attack York (and other historic British cities) in what were known as the Baedeker Raids. At York, its historic buildings, industry and railway were considered as the primary target and both incendiaries and heavy-explosive bombs fell on the station, stables, workshops and the engine sheds. The raid brought about the first withdrawal from the A4 Class, as 4469 *Sir Ralph Wedgewood* was damaged beyond repair. The railway was put back into operation very quickly, but the engine sheds needed much more work. After the end of steam, they later would become the home of the National Railway Museum. In 1962 a visitor to York was this O1 Class 2-8-0 63630 from the ex-Great Central shed at Staveley (41H). Quite what it was doing is not known, but it could well be the working of empty carriage stock from York to Sheffield Victoria just ahead of the summer holiday trains from Britain's 'Steel City'. *John Gill* (E209)

Bottom Left: In 1962 York MPD (50A) provides a home for BR Standard 3MT 2-6-0 77012. Although this was always a North Eastern Region engine, it actually started its life in far away Swindon, where it was built at the old Great Western workshops in the summer of 1954 and supplied to the NER in the second batch of engines from this class. Arguably, if BR had valued its investments of the 1950s in the way the Victorians had viewed theirs, then 77012 could have still been with us today! *John Gill* (B232)

Above: One major Victorian investment, The Great North of England Railway, was the brainchild of North Eastern industrialist Joseph Pease, whose name is most often associated with the Stockton & Darlington. He envisaged a line connecting the York & North Midland with the S&D and then taking this on to Gateshead and Newcastle. In 1835 a line was surveyed from Gateshead to Croft south of Darlington, where it would meet a branch of the S&DR. It was soon realised that the line north of Darlington would be the most difficult to build and it was decided to create the southern end first. Work began on 25th November 1837, and coal traffic began in January 1841; passenger services were instituted four months later.

Over the years that followed, the GNE became part of the ECML, and ahead of World War II important quadrupling and junction improvements were instituted on the section between York and Darlington. It is on that section we see an unusual combination as K1 62044 from Northallerton MPD (51J) heads towards York with a brand new Class 08 diesel shunter, D4169, which is destined for Bristol Bath Road Shed (82A). Some ten months after this May 1962 view, the shed at Northallerton would close and for this reason not many colour photographers visited it. As a consequence, this and many other parts of North Yorkshire are colour photography deserts, if you can help, please let us know!
John Gill (E246)

Above: Leaving York behind, we press now into the West Riding, which has an interesting railway history and will be the subject of a future book in this series. North and east of Leeds, many of the lines were part of the old NER system, and there were few incursions by any other railway. However, the industrialised part of the area was served by a plethora of pre-Grouping companies, including the Great Northern, Hull & Barnsley, Lancashire & Yorkshire, London & North Western, Midland and an amalgam of joint lines. At the heart of this, the cities of Bradford, Wakefield and Leeds all developed into important railway destinations on both north - south and east -west routes. One of the interesting east -west routes was the old L&YR main line that linked the Humber to the Mersey, via Manchester and Wakefield.

At the eastern end of the line to Goole, the L&YR developed both a port and a steamship company, and it is there we see a Locomotive Club of Great Britain rail tour on 6th October 1966. Although 2-8-0s, such as Wakefield's 90076, were commonly used on freight trains, it was not unusual to see them with a rake of coaches. Usually this would be as the result of a failure of another type of engine, but they were often used to handle special trains in peak periods, such as the local summer holidays. Originally based at Newcastle's Heaton Shed (52B) when she came to the LNER after its wartime service, 90076 would eventually end up at Thornaby (51L) until steam was withdrawn in the area. It was finally consigned to Arnott Young's Dinsdale yard in November 1967!

Strathwood Library Collection (B225)

Top Right: As we will be looking at the area in detail in a later book, it is not appropriate to go into the history of the development of local lines. However, it is worth saying that we have now ventured firmly on to Midland Railway metals at Royston. The dampness of Yorkshire is clearly obvious in this May 1967 view, and the misery continued at Royston & Notton, which lost its station at the end of the year. The L&YR station Notton & Royston had closed in April 1966, but coal traffic remained high on both the L&YR and MR lines. Here is one of Stanier's 8F 2-8-0s 48162 on a down coal working, made up of 16-ton steel open wagons with the side doors that were favoured in this part of the region. Many thousands of wagons were built at the Charles Roberts works in nearby Horbury over the years.
J.R. Beddows (M430)

Bottom Right: More clanking and screeching would have been heard by onlookers as 90688 comes to a halt on wet rails after a signal stop at Wakefield Kirkgate on a rainy 13th June 1967. This 2-8-0 had been to more glamorous parts having seen war service in Belgium during 1945, when it was based at Hasselt. It was one of 390 built at the Vulcan Foundry in four large batches. Kirkgate station was built on the L&YR line to Goole and it opened its doors on 15th October 1840, a full 17 years before (what is now) the principal station at Wakefield Westgate. A spur was later built between the two stations, allowing GNR trains access to Kirkgate; both stations remain open today.
J.R. Beddows (B257)

Left: The L&YR engine shed at Wakefield was expanded by the LMS and under BR it became the major shed in the area. When it became part of the North Eastern Region in 1956, it was re-classed as 56A, before being replaced by a modern traction depot at Healey Mills. After 1956 it gained an allocation of ex-LNER types, including the versatile B1 Class 4-6-0s. One of these, 61353, is seen picking up a fireman (complete with a billycan of tea) in October 1964. Although it was an LNER design, this was one of the B1s that were built after nationalisation and before the flow of Standards arrived. When withdrawn from Wakefield, the B1 was to go north to Hughes Bolckow's yard at North Blyth for cutting up in February 1966 after a short working life. *Win Wall, Strathwood Library Collection* (E211)

Above: The availability of late-build engines such as the B1 shown opposite was one of the reasons why the BR Standard 4-6-0s were rare in this region. Even so, the LNER engines were still interlopers to those of us who watched steam in this area, and the favourites remained the Stanier 4-6-0s. The Jubilee Class engines were cherished, and most were well turned out and had shining nameplates, even when cleaners seemed in short supply. A resplendent 45698 *Mars* is seen above whilst conducting an engine change with the preserved K4 Class 3442 *The Great Marquess* in Wakefield. However, just stop to examine the arrangements of pulleys and cranks to work the points and signals that can be seen in the foreground of the picture. *Trans Pennine Archive* (M438)

Left: As will be appreciated, Normanton became a major junction at an early stage with the North Midland (MR), the York & North Midland (NER) and the Manchester & Leeds (L&YR) all meeting here. The L&YR established a major shed here, and after the North East Region was formed it became 55E. Even well into BR days the station and shed were very busy, as Normanton had become known as 'The Crewe of the North'; here one of Wakefield's numerous Austerity 2-8-0s, 90625, winds past the station on the old MR line in May 1967. The coaling tower stands defiantly in the background as a robust lattice gantry, temporarily engulfed in steam, frames the engine.

J.R. Beddows (B268)

Above: Leeds was the ultimate goal of the Manchester & Leeds scheme when it promoted its trans-Pennine line north of Manchester, and crossed the Pennines at Summit. Entering the Calder Valley it served Halifax, Dewsbury and Wakefield, but only got as far as Normanton, where it made contact with the North Midland for the final run to Leeds. Another early line to the city was the Leeds, Dewsbury & Manchester Railway (later LNWR), which took a direct route from Dewsbury. Resting in the city's former Midland shed at Holbeck (55A), Stanier Jubilee 45697 *Achilles* looks down at heel as water drips in through the leaking roof on a rainy July day in 1966.

Win Wall, Strathwood Library Collection (M441)

Above: The city of Bradford was served by two railways, one from the Calder Valley (L&YR) and one from the Aire Valley (MR), followed later by the Great Northern Railway's West Riding lines. The L&YR and GNR both shared the city's Exchange station, where we see a very grimy Fairburn 2-6-4T. Obviously waiting with a portion of a train that will be joined onto a mainline working at Leeds, 42184 carries express lamps although she is to run bunker-first. Even the usually shiny orange enamel station signs have lost all of their lustre in these surroundings. Our photographer recorded the scene for us on the 23rd October 1966. *Dave Hill* (M442)

Right: Politics and finance kept Bradford's two stations apart for many years. When plans were finally made to link Exchange with the Midland Station at Forster Square, they were killed off by World War I and the two, although only a few hundred yards apart, would never be connected! In the less than salubrious surroundings of Bradford Forster Square carriage sidings, we find another Fairburn 2-6-4T, 42093. The scene from 30th April 1966 shows that much-needed but all too often forgotten task of carriages being cleaned and prepared for their next journey, whilst the fireman sorts out his coal bunker.
Win Wall, Strathwood Library Collection (M429)

Above: *At the outset of the book we asked, 'Wouldn't it be wonderful to find a collection of colour pictures on the line up to Alnwick, Wooler and Coldstream? Well, even though Wooler lost its passenger trains in September 1930, this view shows Ivatt 46474 at the town on a rail tour in April 1963.*

Strathwood Library Collection (M427)

EVERY PICTURE is worth a thousand words, or so they say, and thanks to the combined talents of photographers who have supplied material to both the Strathwood and Trans-Pennine archives, we have a lot to say in future volumes. Of course it would not have been possible to tell this story without the kind co-operation of the contributors named in the credits shown in this book.

In conclusion, can we offer a reminder that all of these published shots are available to purchase as superb duplicate slide copies direct from Strathwood. The code number at the end of each slide indicates its catalogue number, and also the name of the photographer whose work we felt warranted inclusion.

To get your copy of the extensive catalogue listing of these and many thousands of other shots available in fabulous colour, please send £5.00 to: -

Strathwood Limited
Kirkland House
Bruce Street, Whithorn.
Dumfries & Galloway DG8 8PY

Or visit the websites: -
www.strathwood.com or www.railwayslide.co.uk.

In return we will send the collector's catalogue, complete with sample slide, post free to UK addresses (overseas add £2.50).